INSTANT

Single

MOM

Praise for Instant Single Mom

"I found this book to be very well thought out, heartfelt, & well written. This book captivated my attention from the very beginning. Being a person that has a very short attention span, this book kept me engaged the entire time. I could not put the book down and that is very rare for me. I could feel every emotion & scenario described as if I were there in this very moment. I think this book can be for those thinking about marriage, married, or widowed. With me being a single woman looking to get married there were several lessons I took from this book. I learned a lot from finances to wedding vows. For example, the "true" meaning of "For Better or Worse, For Richer or Poorer, In sickness and in Health". This book really put these traditional wedding vows into a real-life perspective. These words now have a brand new meaning to me. I now, more than ever, realize that those vows have much deeper meaning than what is on the surface. These are vows that I need to think about way before ever saying I do. I can honestly say this book left me wanting more. I really hope Monica continues this as a sequel."
-Candice Wilson

"I really enjoyed the book Instant Single Mom: This Was Not The Dream. I enjoyed reading the life and love story of Monica and Mike. The story was told so well that you will feel like you're right there on the journey with them. It's a great read and couldn't put it down. This book is great for anyone getting married, thinking of getting married and recently widowed. You will understand what marriage is all about, what it takes, and what it means when you say" for better or for worse" and find encouragement to keep moving if you are a Instant Single Mom as a result of being a widow. I thoroughly enjoyed this book and it left me wanting more. I can't wait for volume 2."

-Jessica Edwards

INSTANT

Single

MOM

THIS WAS NOT THE DREAM

MONICA P. QUINONES

Poised Success
Arlington, VA

Instant Single Mom: This Was Not the Dream
Copyright © 2020 Monica Quinones
Foreword copyright 2020 Kevin G. Swann
Published 2020 by Poised Success

Poised Success
Instagram/poised_success
Facebook/Poised Success
Monicaconsults@poisedsuccess.com

ISBN: 978-0-9972045-1-3

Printed in the United States.

Contact Monica Quinones for speaking engagements at:
  Monicaconsults@poisedsuccess.com
  Instagram/poised_success

This Book Is Dedicated
In Loving Memory
to my husband Michael Quinones
Proverbs 3:5-6 (KJV)

Acknowledgments

First and foremost, I would like to thank God for giving me the comfort, peace, and strength to keep moving forward one moment at a time along my journey. I would like to thank my husband Michael who encouraged and supported me in all my endeavors. He will forever and always be in my heart.

I would like to acknowledge our children, Devin, Mya, and Myles, who have demonstrated strength and encouragement beyond their years during this challenging period.

Words can't express how grateful I am for my parents Wilroy and Carolyn Pretlow, my brother and sister-in-law Roy and Brenda (Farmer) Pretlow, my adopted sister LaChelle Farmer, my adopted niece Shantel Farmer, my adoptive mom Linda Farmer, my father-in-law and mother-in-law Ricardo and Sandra Quinones, my sister-in-laws and brother-in-laws Yvonne and Ramone Williams and Joseph and Jasmin Quinones, my brother-in-law David Quinones, my cousin-in-law Jeffery Scott Van Eyken, and mother-in-law Louise Van Eyken.

I would also like to acknowledge the Farmer, Pretlow, Quinones, Van Eyken, and Washington families.

I would also like to acknowledge a slew of the countless family members and friends who stepped in to help with the kids, came to visit, sent meals, gift cards, and greeting cards, prayed for us, and performed other special acts of kindness for myself, Mike, and the kids. Your kindness does not go unnoticed and is greatly appreciated.

I would like to acknowledge my Pastor Rev. Dr. Kevin Swann and First Lady Tatrece Swann, as well as our church family at Ivy Baptist Church Newport News, VA. I would also like to acknowledge Pastor George and Mrs. Gloria Spicer, and our church family at Christian Union, VA (the church I attended growing up), Senior Pastors Steven and Holly Furtick and Campus Pastors Chad and Jill Hampton at Elevation Church Lake Norman Campus, Charlotte, NC (where we attended in NC), and Oasis Ministry at Lake Forest Church, Huntersville, NC (where I attended bible study classes in NC). We truly appreciate the love you have shown during Michael's sickness and since his passing.

I am also very grateful for the support of Amanda and Mike Sellers, Candice Wilson, Ayana and Methuselah Dixon, Markesha and Rick Farmer Parker,

Toya Critchlow, Alecia and James Foulke, and Liz and Ed Vargas, who assisted with our kids and/or provided us with a place to stay when Mike and I or the kids and I traveled.

I am equally thankful for **ALL** of our prayer warriors. I would have to write a completely separate book to name each and every one of you. We love you ALL so very much! Special thanks to the following individuals who have gone above and beyond during my marriage, throughout Michael's illness, and beyond his transition—Alantha and Harold Gaston, Teresa and Evan Daniels, Janica and Monte Cole, Aleasa Chapman, Aretha and Godfried Yeboah, Lisa and Mark Crump, Tami and Kevin Toms, Monica and Rueben White, Robin and Shawn Overbey, Tabitha and David Person, Mixona and Warren James, Veleka and James Finch, Barbara Smith, Timeka Jordan, Melissa Anderson, Geneva Benjamin, Rachael Ba, Monique and Charles Shier, Major Byrd III, Geneva Henderson, Kenda Claggion, Ericka and Lance Ricks, Aletta Scales, Jessica Edwards, Crystal Sessoms, Valerie and Tony Vasquez, Irreka and Tramarr Knots, Michele Hamm, Mael Brutes, Jill Brewster, Gawaine Hughes, and Janet Legette.

Finally, I would like to give special thanks to the doctors, nurses, and other staff members at Southern

Oncology and Associates, Memorial Sloan Kettering, Duke University Cancer Center, Levine & Dickson Palliative and Hospice Care, and Poole Funeral Home. We are also grateful for the flexibility of management and the support of his colleagues at USAA where Michael was employed.

Table of Contents

Foreword

As a Pastor, I have had the privilege of marrying hundreds of couples. There is a moment in each ceremony where I pause and just look into the eyes of the couple about to be married. Their eyes are usually filled with happiness and joy; there is excitement about having family and friends present to witness a very important moment in their lives. But I also know something full well that the couple may not realize in that moment. After the wedding ceremony is over, they have NO IDEA what could happen to them. Most couples believe that life will be fantastic and that they will live happily ever after. Yet, I know for certain that most couples don't live like that. In fact, that didn't happen to my wife and me (we are now married for over 20 years). What I know to be most true is that life and the people living it can and will change, and that unexpected things can happen.

That's really what this book is about—the understanding that life can be beautiful one day and overwhelming the next; that in life, we can't always anticipate the most difficult experiences that lie ahead. Life is rarely a straight line—rather, it's filled with unexpected twists that can throw us "for a loop." Monica is living proof of this maxim; Michael and Monica were married, had beautiful children, and relocated from Virginia to North Carolina to pursue a "better life." Then the unthinkable happened... Michael was diagnosed with cancer and after a hard-fought battle, he transitioned. Now Monica remains as a young widow and sole caretaker for their children, who are also searching for answers as to why their daddy is no longer here.

While the book will share Michael's and Monica's story, it will also reveal how she has survived the most challenging experience of her life. Like Monica, all of us will have a life-defining moment where neither money, nor material possessions, nor other people will be able to help us. It is in these moments that we must ask ourselves where our REAL source of strength comes from. Who TRULY understands what I'm going through and can help me make sense of it? It is in these moments where we discover how REAL God is—that God is not just a figment of our imaginations or some mystical figure, but is instead who He claims to be: a source of strength, power, and wonder to those who need Him.

To be sure, trusting in God doesn't take all of the pain away. Trusting in God doesn't magically make everything okay. But trusting in God does give us the strength to keep going, even when life doesn't make sense; even when life has thrown us a vicious "curve ball."

I know that this book will be an inspiration to all who read it because what God did (and continues to do) for Monica, He can do for you, too. Unfortunately, pain, heartache, and suffering are all a part of life's journey. They can't always be escaped or avoided. At times, we must face them head on, whether we want to or not. But in these times, just remember Psalm 46:1: "God is our refuge and strength, a very present help in trouble. (NKJV)"

May God give you the strength you need to continue on the path He has assigned for you.

Rev. Kevin G. Swann, D. Min.
Pastor
Ivy Baptist Church
Newport News, VA

Introduction

March 15th, 2004 is a date that I'll never forget. I was surprised when I got a call from Michael that morning telling me not to make any plans for the evening. He also told me that he was taking me out for dinner and to dress for the occasion. Now, I didn't have any problems with dressing up or going out to dinner. I enjoy eating! I just didn't quite feel up to going out this particular evening. I had been busy since the weekend and this was during the middle of the week. Honestly, I was just tired. However, I agreed to go out.

We arrived at Havana Restaurant prior to our reservation time and hung out downstairs near the bar area while we waited to be seated. I enjoyed our conversation, as I normally did. Suddenly, I was startled by one of the waiters when he handed me a dozen roses. Mike told me to read the card, which said, "I can't wait to spend this evening with you. Love Mike." I thought this was so sweet. I thought to myself, *Alright now Mr. Q. I'm glad I decided to come out tonight after all.*

Shortly after I received the roses from the waiter, we were informed that our table was ready. We started walking up a flight of stairs, and at the top we went through a private door where there were tables set up. This area had a more elegant and romantic ambience. There was soft music playing and we were seated at a round table for two, set up with fine linen and amazing table décor. There were only about three other couples in this area, and we were all spread out across the room, giving each couple their own sphere of privacy.

After we placed our order, we began to have a more intimate conversation about our hopes and dreams. We both loved God and we both loved music and writing songs. We had dreams which included helping other people, and we both revered family, sharing other values as well. As our conversation continued, Mike began to share deeper personal things about himself with me. Our food arrived and then Mike stood up from the table. He pulled a small box out of his pocket and got down on one knee. *Y'all*, I don't even remember what he said right after that. I was smiling from ear to ear. Then I heard him ask, "Will you marry me?"

"Yes!" I exclaimed. The other couples and restaurant staff clapped as we kissed. I was too excited to eat my dinner.

Here we were, just the two of us, about to embark on the journey of marriage. I was on cloud nine!! I could just picture our future together. We would build generational wealth, have kids, enjoy watching and helping them grow up to have successful lives of their own, enjoy life with each other, and grow old together. Ahhh yes...that was the dream...

I was beyond excited to tell my family and friends. When I told my parents, they revealed that Mike had asked for my hand in marriage prior to proposing. I was very glad to hear this. Although some may think it very old-fashioned for the man to ask the woman's father for permission to marry his daughter, I believe that some traditions are worth keeping. It was important for me to know that whoever wanted to marry me asked my father to receive his blessing. When I found out Mike had done this with my dad, it sealed the deal even more.

Mike and I agreed to go to pre-marital counseling and had a number of counseling sessions over a four-month period. During counseling we discussed almost everything you could think of. We talked about our credit scores, investments, health insurance, life insurance, car insurance, how many children we wanted to have, what the discipline of the children would look like, how to set boundaries with family and friends, our relationship with God, the importance of being covered and grounded in a good church home, what our giving of our time, talent, and treasure looked like within the church, the importance of sex in the marriage, and communicating through disagreements—the list could go on and on.

I must acknowledge that although Mike and I discussed these topics and concerns before marriage, it was just our representatives sitting in the chairs during those sessions. What do I mean by representatives? I'm glad you asked. By that, I mean that we were just showing the nicer, higher-level sides of ourselves—not our *real* selves. We answered according to what we thought the other person wanted to hear in the moment. We spared feelings at times. We just weren't authentic. I can honestly admit that I was at times more concerned about the wedding ceremony than I was about the longevity of the marriage. Yes, y'all—I know. That was crazy, right? For me, as for many Americans, it was true nonetheless.

Mike and I revisited the discussions we'd had in premarital counseling sessions a few years into our marriage. He told me he didn't want to lose me, so during a lot of those counseling sessions he said what he thought would make me happy. He told me that he valued the idea of being married and that he wanted a life partner but admitted that this was as far as he'd thought it through. In retrospect, Mike and I both agreed that we shouldn't have gotten married at the time that we did. We both agreed that we should have worked on some of our individual shortcomings and laid out how we truly felt about certain topics discussed in counseling. These issues didn't mean that we shouldn't have gotten married at all, just that we both needed to grow in certain areas before saying "I do" to the lifelong commitment of marriage.

Based on the high number of divorces in our country, I can say that Mike and I, at the time of marriage counseling, were not unique. Experience taught us that it is important not only to go to premarital counseling, but also to be honest within your courtship and recognize where you *really* are as a couple before marriage. Marriage is not a career. If you don't like it, you don't get to just quit it and move on to the next without any consequences. In a career, you ultimately have the right to leave the company at any time and the company can similarly let you go at any given time. In a marriage you can leave, however there are legal matters that have to be discussed and resolved before the marriage can end. I encourage you to take your time and be honest with yourself before saying "I do." Not being completely true to ourselves contributed to a lot of disagreements and misunderstandings during our first few years of our marriage. Fortunately, with God's help we survived!

During our wedding ceremony Mike and I said the traditional wedding vows: "for better or worse, for richer or poorer, through sickness and in health, 'til death do we part." Standing there at the altar and saying those vows, I didn't truly realize how all-encompassing they were. Yes, I knew that marriage could and would have its testing and trying moments, but in my mind, we would just overcome them with a great attitude and move forward. Ha!...Y'all—oh my goodness. I'm so grateful for an evolved perspective. Whew! In any marriage, you cannot know what the "for worse," "for poorer," or "in sickness" will really entail. You definitely don't know when the "til death do we part" will come. You're not even thinking about that part of your vows. Mike and I weren't either. Little did we know that we would live out all of our vows with their accompanying highs and lows and that "til death do we part" would come at a time when we thought we were just getting started.

In this book, Instant Single Mom: This Was Not the Dream, I will offer you a glimpse into my marriage with Mike. I will let you in to see some of the challenges and the good times we had together. My goals here are to give you some things to think about before marriage, encouragement to endure in your marriage, and hope to move forward when the last part of the vows manifests itself in reality and not just in words spoken during the marriage ceremony.

Now, go and grab a cup of coffee, tea, soda, wine, or whatever it is that you would like to drink. Settle into your favorite spot at home or wherever it is that you like to go when you read. Come in and have a seat at my table. Turn the page.

Right There

...So brokenhearted and filled with so much pain
I prayed to my father to show me love again
And then when I turned it over
He showed me so much more
'cause right there in the midst of it all
An angel appeared before.

Right there in the midst of,
In the midst of my storm,
God sent to me an angel
And showed me love once more.
Right there in the midst of the,
Midst of my storm,
God sent to me an angel
And you appeared before...

Monica Pretlow Quinones

Chapter 1

May 14th, 2005: Our Dreams Became A Reality

"And now I present to you, for the first time, Mr. and Mrs. Michael Quinones!" the DJ announced loudly in the microphone. Our families and friends cheered and clapped as Mike and I entered the ballroom for our wedding reception. All eyes were on us as we began to dance to our first song as husband and wife: "Spend My Life with You" by Eric Benet (featuring Tamia). We both loved that song. For our 12th wedding anniversary years later, I made a video with that song playing in the background. It was a great anniversary gift and Mike loved it.

Yes, I was one of those girls who, for as long as I can remember, dreamed of being married. When I was younger, I liked watching movies where the woman married the man she loved or at least where you could put two and two together and the plot led the audience to believe that if the story continued, that's what would happen (movies like *Love Jones* and *Love and Basketball,* for instance).

Later in life I remember praying to God for my husband find me. Seven years later my prayers were answered. I got the man and a bonus child (Mike had a child from his previous marriage)!! Yaassss!! We went on to have two kids from our union, purchased our house, and kept good jobs. We were living the American Dream—as society would call it. Every day wasn't your romantic fairytale lifestyle, of course. However, on the whole, it was great for us. The good days outweighed the bad. We had a lot of dreams. We both wanted to see those dreams come to pass.

Remembering our dreams was part of what kept us together during the tough times. Our intimacy deepened. We could be vulnerable with one another. Sometimes we were at our worst, but we pushed through, realizing that neither of us was perfect. We had to learn to communicate effectively with one another.

Effective communication plays such a big part in the survival of your marriage. Just because you like to be communicated to in one way doesn't mean that your spouse desires to be communicated to in the same manner. It really is the little things that can make or break a marriage. Learn your partner and learn yourself. When your spouse gets angry, do they like to talk right away, or do they need time alone to gather their composure and thoughts? When giving marital advice, you may have heard people say never to go to bed angry. Well… I don't agree with that advice. Hear me out! Speaking from personal experience, sometimes it was best to just go to sleep. In the morning, both of us had time to rest and gather our thoughts. We learned that when there was a disagreement, we needed to keep the main goal top of mind. The main goal was to come to a place where the matter would be resolved. We also had to learn to truly forgive and move forward. We decided that once a matter was resolved; we couldn't bring it up again in a future disagreement unless it was coming from a positive perspective.

Be intentional about creating moments to just laugh and be weird or silly. Thank your spouse for providing for the family. Pray for your spouse. Choose to be gentle in your response when you really want to respond harshly. For most couples, an unexpected kiss, laughter, affirmation, quality time, gentleness, or sexual connection can trigger a great day, even in the toughest of situations.

Respect your spouses. Ladies—it's so important for

us to show our husbands respect. It's okay to say and be the "S" word. Submissive. Yes, I said submissive. Being submissive is a great thing. Now, I'm not talking about staying in toxic relationships. I'm simply saying that we should submit to our husbands' authority as the heads of our households. We wives must recognize that God's got us covered. He has ordained the order of marriage. I Peter 3:1-7 (NIV) states:

> *Wives, in the same way submit yourselves to your own husbands so that, if any of them do not believe the word, they may be won over without words by the behavior of their wives, when they see the purity and reverence of your lives. Your beauty should not come from outward adornment, such as elaborate hairstyles and wearing of gold jewelry or fine clothes. Rather, it should be that of your inner self, the unfading beauty of a gentle and quiet spirit, which is of great worth in God's sight. For this is the way the holy women of the past who put their hope in God used to adorn themselves. They submitted themselves to their own husbands, like Sarah, who obeyed Abraham and called him her lord. You are her daughters if you do what is right and do not give way to fear. Husbands, in the same way be considerate as you live with your wives and treat them with respect as the weaker partner and as heirs with you of the gracious gift of life, so that nothing will hinder your prayers."*

You see—submission works both ways. Be open to it.

It's a process.

Marriage is work and its worth the work. When you humble yourself and allow God in, He has ways of moving in your relationship that far outweigh anything you could imagine for your marriage.

In sickness and in health. This is part of the traditional marriage vows. I know some of you may have written your own marriage vows, and that's great. Nevertheless, this phrase right here is still something to think about. Have you married someone or are you about to marry someone who you know loves you to the point of staying with you when you get sick? Don't answer this question too quickly. There are many individuals out there that truly cannot handle seeing someone they're in a relationship with go through an illness. They run away, leaving the ill partner to fend for themselves. I thank God that Mike and I were committed to each other in this manner.

During our first year of marriage, after I gave birth to our daughter, I became very ill. I ended up staying in the hospital for about twelve days after giving birth. For a few days, the doctors didn't know what the problem was. I had lost a lot of blood during labor, leading to an emergency c-section and I had to undergo two blood transfusions. The results from a CT scan showed that I had developed a large blood clot under the second layer of the incision from the caesarean. My doctor told me that I needed to undergo surgery right away or I was at risk of cardiac failure and even death. I had the surgery, and after returning to my room in the hospital I went into cardiac arrest. Yes, my heart stopped beating. I woke up to a team of doctors. Thank God for healing me!!! Mike stayed with me every night in the hospital. He could have easily left because our newborn was discharged from the hospital before I was. Fortunately, my parents lived nearby and were able to take care of our daughter at their home. Nonetheless, the fact that Mike stayed with me every night during this ordeal meant a lot to me. When fear would try to creep into my thoughts and spoken words, Mike was there to encourage me and hold my hand.

Seven years later I was involved in a car accident. The effects of this incident resulted in injuries that progressively deteriorated to the point that I could not walk on my own without the use of a walker. This situation lasted about nine months. I was unable to work during this period, so times were financially tight for us. I was dependent on Mike and others to take me to doctor's appointments and other places. By this time, we had our son and he was a toddler. Mike took on majority of the household tasks such as cooking, washing dishes, cleaning, laundry, taking the kids to school, and picking them up from aftercare, etc. This was ministry to me. Ministry? Yes, ministry. You see, shortly before I experienced the car accident, something happened in our marriage that was essentially the last straw for me, leading me to seek legal counsel. I had an attorney draw up separation documents that were ultimately intended to lead to an official divorce.

Mike could tell that I wasn't happy and took the initiative to schedule a counseling session with our pastor. Side note: y'all, that counseling session was all to pieces! A complete mess! Looking back, I can laugh about it now, but at the time…whew! Chile, it was no laughing matter. During the counseling session I informed Mike that I had spoken with an attorney to have separation papers drawn up. Although he knew I was extremely upset, he wasn't expecting this. Mike had already been through one divorce. In the beginning of our union we both agreed that we would not divorce no matter what; however, I was willing to throw in the towel.

Our pastor suggested that we live separately within our home for 60 days while going to marriage counseling. Honestly, when the pastor said this I thought it was the silliest thing I had ever heard. Mike agreed to try while I just sat there (probably looking crazy because I don't have a poker face—what I'm thinking usually shows); but I finally agreed.

During those 60 days I began to see a change in our relationship. Mike fought to save his marriage and our family. This increased my desire to fight for our marriage as well. What I initially thought was ridiculous advice from our pastor turned out to be a pivotal point in the right direction for our marriage.

Right as the 60 days were coming to a close, my nine-month journey of not being able to walk without assistance began. As I mentioned previously, Mike took on a lot of the responsibilities of the household during this time. God literally had me sit still so I could watch my husband. Mike wasn't doing these things simply because I couldn't do them. He was doing these things out of love. I saw glimpses of Mike's relationship with God as it began to grow and become stronger. Mike was being submissive to God and in turn being submissive to me. You see—I told you, being submissive works both ways in a marriage.

A little over a year later, after God healed our marriage and physically healed me such that I could walk again without assistance, our pastor asked if Mike and I would be willing to share our testimony on Resurrection

Sunday (Easter) with the congregation. Mike and I agreed without hesitation. On that particular Sunday, we shared our testimony with over 2,000 people. Wow! You never know what life has in store for you. However, God does. God used a difficult time in our marriage to bless us so that our story could, in turn, be used to help others.

Life

Life is just one long dream
And
Heaven is reality.
In life
We travel along, finding answers to circumstances
and with God's help we put the pieces together
just like we do in a dream
Then,
Suddenly, in the twinkling of an eye,
We awaken in the presence of God.
In the presence of the one who held us, comforted
us, caressed us, and blessed us.
Oh, just to feel Him
And to look upon His face!
Finally,
There is no more sickness, no more pain, no more
heartache, no more frustration, no more envying,
no more strife, no more jealousy, no more mur-
dering,
Or deceit
But
There is love, joy, peace, gentleness, kindness,
meekness,
And best of all, no more tears.
All of this will last eternally

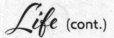 (cont.)

So
Don't cry for me when the alarm clock rings, and
I awaken in my heavenly home.
What you see is the continuation of your dream
and the beginning of my reality.
Remember not to let go of God's hands
Because
He is the key to
Your
Reality!

Monica Pretlow Quinones

Chapter 2

February 23rd, 2019: Shattered Dreams

"Come on, let's go guys!" I said. Getting my kids up and moving has always been a real challenge on the weekends. I'm sure that there are quite a few of you who can relate to that. I decided to turn on the TV and pop some Eggo waffles in the toaster. Of course, as soon as the waffles were ready to eat, the kids were ready to go. Classic. If I had a dollar for every time that happened, I'd be rich! "Let me just eat this real quick and then we can go." I said.

"Okay!" they both replied in unison.

"Are y'all hungry now or do y'all want to stop and grab something on the way to see Daddy?"

My son said, "I already ate but, I could eat again."

My daughter said, "I'm not hungry." I just shook my head and smiled. I could virtually lip sync their very typical responses while they answered the question.

I took two bites from my waffles and then my phone rang. It was 9:45 a.m. The caller ID listed the number of the hospice house. I took a deep breath and answered the phone. "Hello?"

"Hello, may I speak with Mrs. Quinones?" said a woman with a soft-spoken voice.

"This is she" I said.

"Mrs. Quinones, this is Sandy, one of the nurses attending to your husband. We have noticed a significant change in his breathing. You should come right away."

"Okay, I'm on my way." I threw the waffles in the trash.

"Come on, let's go! Grab your coats, let's go." I urged the kids.

They grabbed their things and went out the door to get into the car. My hands started to shake as I barely managed to lock the front door. Mike had chosen to be under a DNR (Do Not Resuscitate) order, which meant that by law, the hospice nurses and doctors could not perform CPR on Mike. I didn't want Mike to choose a DNR status, but I agreed to respect his wishes. I got in the car and sped off. We lived about 30 minutes from the hospice house my husband was in because the one closest to us was full.

I begin to think about what I said to Mike yesterday

afternoon. "Don't worry. The time will go by fast and you'll be back home before you know it." Mike nodded his head in agreement and began to stare past me. Those were the words that I said to Michael as we waited for the transportation service to arrive at our house. Michael was going to be taken to the local hospice house to be provided 24-hour care over the weekend. We were told that this would be temporary. Now, all I could envision in my mind was the transportation person pulling Mike out of the front door to our house in his wheelchair. I made sure that Mike was bundled up with his hat, scarf, gloves, and coat. Mike's feet and legs were very swollen. For the first time I couldn't find any shoes that could fit his feet. God always has a ram in the bush! My cousins (my cousin and her husband. In my family once you marry, we consider them to be a cousin too) were at our house visiting from Virginia to check on Mike (we lived in North Carolina). My cousin happened to have these huge dinosaur slippers he had gotten from somewhere that I don't remember , but they were big enough to get on Mike's feet! I remember standing in the front door-way and Mike was looking back at me wearing those big dinosaur slippers. I smiled. I said, "See you soon. I'm going to get the kids out of school early and we'll be right there."

Mike said, "Okay."

Today was February 22nd. I realized that the next day would mark exactly nine months from the date we received his cancer diagnosis. Nine months—the time it takes a woman to birth a child. Hmmm... Maybe that next day would be the day that God would birth a miraculous healing for Mike. We strongly desired Mike's healing on Earth. Mike and I envisioned us traveling the world to share his testimony. We pictured people confessing their salvation and committing their lives to God. What a powerful testimony it would be for our children to witness. Mike and I prayed together daily. We encouraged each other.

The kids and I went straight to the hospice house. I was so focused on getting there that I didn't think to get the kids and myself something to eat. We were able to get some snacks out of the vending machine but that wasn't dinner. We stayed with Mike until after nine that evening. It was a quiet peaceful night. Mike seemed calm and drifted in and out of sleep due to the medicine he was taking. We prayed together. He kept his faith. We were still trusting in and hoping for God to heal. I wished we could stay over night but that wasn't an option with the kids. Mike understood. Before leaving, the kids gave him hugs and proclaimed, "Love you daddy!"

"Love y'all too," said Mike.

I gave him a bunch of kisses on his forehead (he liked that) and said, "I love you. We'll be back in the morning to spend the entire day with you."

Mike responded, "Okay. I love you too. Thank you. Love you."

I replied, "Get some rest." Mike nodded his head.

SON: "Mommy who was on the phone? Why are you driving so fast?"

ME: "It was the nurse calling about daddy," I said calmly. I knew I had to keep it together for the kids.

DAUGHTER: "What happened?"

ME: "I'm not quite sure. Just trying to get there."

I looked through the rear-view mirror and my son looked scared. I looked to my right and my daughter looked scared also. I didn't have any words of comfort for them now. I began to pray internally to God. God please...please help us. Don't take their dad. Please don't take my husband. Please....please God don't do this.... I don't know what to do.... talk to me God....be with Mike....we need you to heal him now.... you have all power to do it.... please just don't take him........but God....I know it's not about my will and what I want.... you have the final say.... not my will Lord....your will be done.

As I finished praying, I looked at the clock in the car. It was exactly 10 a.m. We were stopped at a traffic light and I decided to go through it.

"Mom!!" both kids yelled.

"It's ok. If we get pulled over, I'll explain this is an emergency." The closer we got to the hospice house, the harder and faster my heart was beating. I started taking deep breaths in through my nose and exhaling out of my mouth. Finally, we arrived at the hospice house. I pulled into a parking space at 10:05 a.m. Yes, I was truly speeding.

We all got out of the car quickly and ran towards the doors. As soon as we got inside, Sandy*, the nurse, met us right at the door and said the words that no one wants to hear about their sick loved one.

"I'm so sorry. He's gone." My heart began to beat even faster. I dropped my purse and began to run around the oval shaped nurses' station to get to Mike's room. I didn't make it. My legs gave out and I fell on the floor. The adrenaline of emotions began to stir. From the pit of my stomach I started hollering and screaming.

"Noooooo! Noooooo! No! No! No! GOD noooo!!! I want my husband back!! I want my husband back!!!

Come back Mike!!!! Come back!!! Come back!!! God why!!!" I shouted these words through my tears. I could hear my kids screaming and crying. I will never ever forget the sound of their piercing screams. Their screams echoed the stabbing pains I felt in my own heart. I wanted to get to my kids and comfort them but I just couldn't get up. A team of nurses surrounded me and the kids.

I don't know how long I laid on the floor crying. Eventually, with the help of the nurses I got up to go into the room with Mike. The kids didn't want to come with me. That walk to his room felt like the longest walk I had ever taken, although it was probably less than 50 feet away. I walked towards Mike's body. He laid on the bed on his back with his mouth wide open. I touched his right hand with my right hand and his forehead with my left hand. His forehead felt warm but his hands were getting colder by the minute. From behind me, the nurse said they had pronounced him deceased at 10 a.m. I just couldn't believe it. "Deceased? No." I started crying again. "Deceased...10 a.m... deceased." I squeezed Mike's hand hoping that he would squeeze mine in return. I remembered that 10 a.m. was the time I had finished my prayer to God in the car. I leaned forward to kiss Mike on the forehead and then I laid my left cheek on his forehead. I cried and cried.

Just like that, in an instant, I became a widow and a single mother. On Saturday, February 23rd. *What in the world? How was I going to get through this? Why did this happen to us? Why?* I couldn't wrap my mind around it. I must have zoned out for a while because I heard the nurse calling my name, "Mrs. Quinones? Mrs. Quinones?" Then she touched me on my arm. "Mrs. Quinones. We have to ask you some questions now. You can take your time responding. Do you have a funeral home in mind? We can't have the body here for longer than a few hours. If you have a funeral home in mind, they will know what to do and we can direct most of our questions to them.

I said, "Funeral home? Ummm...yes. I don't know the name of it right now. My cousin works for a funeral home. I will use that one." As long as I had known the name of the funeral home, I just couldn't think of it at that moment. I must have looked clueless because the nurse put her clipboard down and held my hand. Another nurse walked in and looked at me with concern.

"Mrs. Quinones, my name is Laura*. I have been sitting with your kids. Don't worry they're not alone. We have other nurses out there with them. I just came in to check on you."

"How are my kids?" I inquired.

Nurse Laura said, "As good as can be expected for a time like this."

"Thank you. May I ask you something? How did it happen?"

Nurse Laura replied, "I came in at 8:30 a.m. to check Michael's vitals. He was coherent and answered my questions. I left the room to check on other patients."

Nurse Sandy continued, "I came into the room at 9 a.m. to give him his medicine. He was coherent. I told him that the medicine may make him drowsy. I told him I would be back to check on him and he said okay. I returned to the room at 9:43 a.m. I noticed that his breathing was different. I called for Nurse Laura to return to check his vitals and then I called you at 9:45 a.m. I returned to the room and told Michael that you were on your way. He smiled. Then he closed his eyes and his breathing became slower and shallower. We stayed right here with him. His breathing completely stopped at exactly 10 a.m. He went very peacefully. That doesn't happen for everyone. Hopefully, in the weeks and months to come that will bring you some comfort. We're so sorry."

"Thank you for letting me know. If only we had gotten here sooner..." I lamented.

Nurse Laura said, "Sometimes, when our loved ones transition and we're not with them, it's because they don't want us to see them go. It's almost as if they just want to spare us the pain of them leaving." I nodded my head in agreement. I thought to myself that maybe this was true; but this was not the dream. This was not our dream. Mike and I had so many things left that we wanted to do individually, together, and with our kids. We had high school and college graduations to look forward to; witnessing our kids getting married; witnessing the kids having kids of their own; traveling the world together. The list goes on and on. It just wasn't supposed to end this way. Not from my perspective.

I left the room to be with the kids and to begin to make phone calls. The nurses and staff sat with us and asked the necessary questions in order to start making arrangements for Michael. I am so grateful for all of the family and friends who showed up at the hospice house and called with condolences that day. It was such an outpouring of love.

The nurses advised me to return to the room with Michael because they were going to do a memorial service. The funeral home attendant had arrived and they would be taking Mike to the funeral home in Virginia. I asked the kids and the family and friends who were present if they wanted to go into the room. No one wanted to go. When I entered, I noticed that they had changed

Mike's clothes and put a prayer shawl over him from the middle of his chest down to his feet. As I walked closer, I noticed they had closed his mouth (I tried to do it earlier, but it wouldn't stay closed). What I saw next stopped me in my tracks. Mike had a smile on his face. I walked closer and said to the nurses, "He's smiling."

"Yes, he is, said Nurse Laura. "He went peacefully. I truly believe your husband is in God's presence."

I sighed as tears began to form and said, "I do too."

The nurses led the memorial service and prayed with us. When we were done, the funeral home attendant came in to roll Mike's body out on the gurney and the nurses gently pulled the prayer shawl up to his neck. They handed me some flowers to lay on top of him, which I placed on his stomach. We walked behind the funeral attendant until they rolled Mike out of the building. This was just so unreal…SO…UN…REAL.

Dear God, Please help me trust you Through the unexpected Turns of life

Isaiah 40:31(NIV) *"...but those who hope in the Lord will renew their strength. They will soar on wings like eagles; they will run and not grow weary; they will walk and not be faint."*

Chapter 3

May 23rd, 2018: The Beginning of Our Battle

"Hello!" I answered happily. I was singing and dancing to the music playing in the car while I was driving.

"Hey—I need you to come home right away," said Mike. I detected a note of concern in his voice and I paused. I could tell that something was wrong.

"Okay. I'm coming," I said.

Mike responded, "Okay."

I hung up the phone and began to drive home. I began to talk to God. The test results must be in. Right, God? I paused. Then I sensed the Spirit telling me to stay calm and strong for him. I could feel the tears forming but then I took a deep breath and said out loud, "Okay. Okay. I will." I began to repeat softly, "I can do all things through Christ who strengthens me. I can do all things through Christ who strengthens me.

I can do all things through Christ who strengthens me."
(Philippians 4:13 NKJV)

I arrived at home safely, took a deep breath, and unlocked the door. Mike was crying. I went over to him and gave him a long hug. We didn't speak for a few minutes. Then Mike said, "Mon (he called me Mon – short for Monica), the biopsy results came back and I have a rare form of cancer." Mike wept some more in my arms. Then he spoke again, "It's called Cholangiocarcinoma. I had never even heard of it before. I looked it up and it says it's terminal. I have to meet with an oncologist and discuss possible treatment options." Mike cried some more.

I said, "Don't worry. God is with us. God has you. We're going to fight this!" I stepped back from him, wiped his tears with my fingers, and looked him in his eyes. "Do you hear me? We're going to fight this!" He stopped crying and said, "Okay." He proceeded to get on the phone and make some calls. I left the room and went into the bathroom to pray.

Telling the Kids

"How are we going to tell the kids?" I asked Mike.

He paused and said, "I don't want to tell them I have cancer." Another longer pause.

"We have to tell them. They're very smart and observant. They will pick up that something is wrong," I reminded him. Mike sat down in his desk chair. We often had our most important conversations in this room with the door closed.

"Alright, let's tell them when they get home from school. I won't tell them it's cancer, though. I'll tell them that my liver is sick and I'm doing everything in my power to fight it," Mike resolved.

"I don't agree with that, Mike. I know this is a lot to process but they should know the whole truth. What if they overhear a conversation or see paperwork or see side effects from treatment?" I asked.

"We will cross that bridge when it's necessary. I don't want to worry them," Mike asserted. I paused and looked down at the floor. In my heart I didn't agree but I didn't want to keep going back and forth about it.

I yielded only slightly. "Okay. My okay is just an I hear what you're saying. I will respect your decision. But I don't agree with it completely."

Mike said, "Okay. Thank you."

When the kids came home from school, Mike and I sat them down and had the conversation. Mike did most of the talking. The expressions on their faces were a combination of fear and concern. I could tell that our daughter knew there was more to the story, but she didn't ask more questions then. Both kids gave Mike very long hugs. I had to fight back the tears. Due to uncontrollable circumstances, we had to tell our oldest child over the phone. Mike informed him of the actual diagnosis. That was heartbreaking.

The weeks went by and the actual cancer diagnosis wasn't fully discussed with the younger kids. The side effects of the chemotherapy treatment began to show through Mike's energy levels, stomach issues, and some weight loss. One day, as we were on our way home in the car, I pulled up to the mailbox and I asked our daughter to get the mail. She looked at the mail as she was taking it out. I could tell by the look on her face that something was wrong. When she handed me the mail, I noticed that there was something from the American Cancer Center addressed to Mike. Just like that, exactly what I was concerned would happen, did. When we walked into the house, our daughter went to her room and I immediately told Mike what happened. Mike told the kids that day and it was devastating for all of us.

What is Cholangiocarcinoma?

Just like Mike, I hadn't heard of Cholangiocarcinoma. According to the Mayo Clinic, Cholangiocarcinoma is a form of cancer that starts in the slender tubes (bile ducts) that carry the digestive fluid bile. Bile ducts connect your liver to your gallbladder and your small intestine. Some people also refer to this as bile duct cancer. Research shows that this type of cancer is uncommon and typically occurs in people aged 50 and older, however, there have been cases—like Michael's—where younger people have had the disease. Michael was 49 at the time of his diagnosis. According to the Mayo Clinic research, Cholangiocarcinoma is a very difficult type of tumor to treat. As with any form of cancer, the sooner it is detected, the greater chance of survival. When Mike was diagnosed, the cancer was at a stage IV. Research from Memorial Sloan Kettering Cancer Center states that bile duct cancer is usually asymptomatic until it reaches an advanced stage and has spread to other organs and tissues.

I often get asked the questions like, "What caused this type of cancer?" "What were the symptoms?" According to research at the Mayo Clinic, Cholangiocarcinoma occurs when cells in the bile ducts develop changes (mutations) in their DNA—the material that provides instructions for every chemical process in your body. DNA mutations cause changes in the instructions. One result is that cells may begin to grow out of control and eventually form a tumor — a mass of cancerous cells. It's not clear what causes the genetic mutations that lead to cancer. Signs and symptoms of Cholangiocarcinoma include:

- Yellowing of your skin and the whites of your eyes (jaundice)
- Intensely itchy skin
- White-colored stools
- Fatigue
- Abdominal pain
- Unintended weight loss

On our first visit with the oncologist, the doctor informed Mike that there was nothing he did to cause this type of cancer. From our conversation and the types of questions we were asking, the doctor could tell that we were searching for clues as to what may have contributed to this disease. Mike wasn't a smoker, he wasn't a heavy drinker, he hadn't been overseas or come in contact with any disease-causing parasites. These were just some of the things our own Internet research on the possible causes of this disease suggested. The fact that we were even sitting in an oncologist's office and discussing treatment plans for this type of cancer was mind-blowing to me and Mike. We were definitely reaching and searching for answers and ways to fight the disease, both medically and spiritually.

Spiritual Transformation

May 23rd, 2018, to February 23rd, 2019, was a period of exactly nine months. Wow. The same amount of time it takes for human life to bloom. During this period, I watched my husband of almost 14 years go from being about 240 pounds down to about 145 pounds. There is nothing worse—and I do mean *nothing* worse—than watching someone you truly love and care about become very ill and begin to waste away. I felt so helpless. I wanted to fix Mike and make him 120% better. This, however, was totally out of my human control. Mike and I had to truly give it to God. In doing this, I was able to see past the outward decline of his body and into the aura of his soul. Michael had grown so much in his spiritual walk with God during this trial. His growth in God had a domino effect in me that persuaded me to strengthen and grow deeper in my own faith. You see, I watched this man grow spiritually, right before my very eyes.

When I first met Michael, I knew he was saved. "Saved," meaning that he professed his belief in and love for Christ. He would speak about God. He would go to church on occasion. He would even give offerings when he attended. Between you and me, we both know that doing these things doesn't mean that a person truly has a relationship with God. We're all at different stages of our walks with God along this journey of life. So, don't get me wrong. I'm not sharing this as a form of judgement against my husband or anyone else. I'm simply painting the picture of where he was at the beginning of our relationship and the extent to which he evolved.

We went through some challenging times in our marriage. Truth be told, we didn't *really* keep God at the center of our relationship. During year seven, we really hit a wall. It was then that I sought legal counsel to file for separation. This was a wakeup call for both Michael and I. He truly fought for our marriage and to keep our family together. We went through counseling, attended church more frequently together, and prayed together. Fortunately, things took a turn for the better. With God, supportive family, our pastor, the marriage ministry at church, and our friends, we were able to grow, move forward, and rebuild our relationship. Michael truly loved me and the kids. I'm so grateful that we were able to stay together—and not in misery, nor just for the sake of our kids—because we allowed God to have his way in our individual lives and in our marriage.

Here we were five years later, and another health challenge had occurred. This time it was Mike who fell ill. I became the caregiver. I went to all of his treatments and doctor's appointments near and far. I took care of him and the kids. I was up with him late at night into the early morning hours. I took care of him when he would vomit from the side effects of treatment or just from his illness. I would rub and scratch his back frequently due to itchy skin from the cancer. I ran all errands for him. The list was endless. However, I wouldn't have had it any other way. If it meant that I had to take care of him in that manner until we grew old together, I would have. THAT is love.

I can honestly say that I loved Mike more on the day he passed away than I did the day we were married. Why do I say that? It's because on the day we got married, I didn't really know what being married was all about. Yes, we went through pre-marital counseling. Yes, we knew we loved each other on the surface. Yes, we desired to have a great marriage. Yes, we knew if the marriage were to be successful, we needed to keep God in it. Still, we had no idea what we were about to get into. When two people get married, it is literally the coming together of two worlds. But the beginning of our marriage didn't have the level of depth that it had grown to by the time of Mike's transition. Through all our trials and circum-stances; through the great times and the not so great times, our love grew deeper and more intimate in ways that, at the most difficult moments in our marriage, I never thought possible.

Do you see how important it is for you to truly think about who you're marrying? That person needs to be committed to weathering the storms of life with you. They also need to be committed to growing with God individually. As your partner's relationship with God grows, positive change within your marriage will manifest.

I loved and continue to love my husband. I miss cooking for him. I miss laughing with him. I miss watching him with our kids. No, he wasn't perfect; but he was perfect for us. Enjoy your spouse. Don't waste time on being at odds with one another. Value each other. None of us knows how long we have with our spouse when we get married. We may know our birth dates, but only God knows our end dates. What do you think could happen within our marriages if we reminded ourselves of this reality each day?

I know and believe that when trials or challenging circumstances arise, they intentionally occur to make us stronger. I've seen it happen in my own life plenty of times. I have also seen it happen in the lives of others. However, sometimes a challenge can arise that just knocks the wind out of you! You know? I believe that when this happens, God has us right where He wants us.

Completely dependent upon Him so He can comfort and guide us.

That is exactly what Mike and I set out to do. We gave God glory despite our circumstances. We had grown through previous experiences in our marriage and through some of my own health challenges. Therefore, we knew God was a healer because we had experienced it firsthand. Yes, this was scary for us in our natural human state; but knowing God as our Father, we knew there was nothing too hard for Him. All things are possible with God.

We were surrounded by family, friends, church family, co-workers, nursing staff, doctors, and sometimes even strangers who encouraged Mike, the kids, and me. Mike and I prayed together. We even had an ongoing group text messaging conversation between Mike and I and seven other family members. Mike sent devotionals to us daily which was meant to lift our spirits and provide a space of support and refuge. The devotionals Mike sent were a way to encourage us and Mike too. This was truly amazing to witness because it speaks to his growth with God despite the current circumstances he was facing.

During his chemotherapy treatments, Mike made friends with the nurses and the staff. He even made friends with and prayed for the other patients undergoing treatment. For instance, there were a mother and her son there. We learned that the mom was diagnosed with lung cancer and that it had spread throughout her body. Her son faithfully brought her in for all of her treatments. He shared with us that his father—also his mother's husband—had passed away from lung cancer just a few years prior. Mike and I could sense how scared the son was, having to watch his mother battle the same illness. I watched Mike as he encouraged both the mother and the son. We prayed for them often. Then one day, the mom told Mike that her recent scan showed no evidence of cancer in her body. Only scars where the cancer use to be. We all praised God for her miraculous healing!! What an amazing testimony!!! I was so happy for them. Mike and I were encouraged by this miracle and testimony. It gave us so much hope. We believed in our hearts that God could heal Mike of this terminal illness.

Shortly after hearing the testimony of this miraculous event, Mike begin to see the specialist at Sloan Kettering in New York more frequently. He pursued treatment with renewed vigor. The smaller tumors were beginning to grow while the large tumor remained the same size, so Mike decided to participate in a clinical trial. Before he could fully participate in the trial however, he had to go through extensive physical observation to ensure that his body could handle the treatment. While these tests were being completed, the doctors informed Michael that he could not receive any chemotherapy so that his body could prepare itself to handle the pill from the clinical trial. By this time, it was November. We had just flown back home to North Carolina from New York when Mike received a phone call from the doctor's office informing him that his liver enzymes were too high for him to participate in the trial. Talk about being devastated. I kept it together to allow Mike to focus on his own emotions, but internally I was heartbroken. We asked more questions and they advised us of our last option, which was to insert a pump about the size of a hockey puck into Mike's body that could send treatment directly to the tumors.

Mike was sad, however he continued to trust God and so did I. We didn't have much time and needed to make a decision. After prayer and research, Mike made a brave choice and decided to participate in a clinical trial that would require him to undergo major surgery. The clinical trial involved removing Mike's gallbladder and inserting a digital pump about the size of a hockey puck into him on the left side of his abdomen. The pump would receive the chemotherapy medicine and then send the drugs directly to the tumors in and on his liver. The gallbladder was removed so that it wouldn't block the flow of the medicine going directly to the tumors. This surgery was nothing to take lightly. Michael was scheduled to stay in the hospital for five days. We had to make arrangements for the kids. Fortunately, the doctors in New York told us that the surgery could be done at Duke University Hospital in North Carolina, which was great news because we would be at least in the same state as our children.

The surgery was scheduled for December 12th. We were so grateful for the friends and family that came together to help with the kids and provide us with cooked food during this time. I was also very grateful for my parents, who rearranged their schedules to drive three and a half hours to be with me and Mike. I can't even begin to tell you how much that meant to both of us. I would have been a nervous wreck for sure sitting in the waiting room by myself while Mike was having surgery.

At first things looked great. The surgery went well. The doctor reported that the cancer hadn't metastasized—meaning that it hadn't spread anywhere else—in Mike's body. Things seemed to be going in the right direction. He had even gotten out of the bed to practice walking around with the nurse. Then suddenly, things seemed to take a turn for the worse. Mike's body began to decline. He ended up in the hospital for nine days, but we were grateful that he was discharged in time to spend Christmas at home.

The kids were so excited to have all of us together for Christmas. I wanted the holidays to be special this year more than ever. Since moving to North Carolina, we traditionally went home to Virginia to spend the holidays with family. When we had moved, we had to leave all of our Christmas decorations—including the Christmas tree—behind, because there was nowhere to store those items at our new place. Christmas was just a few days away, so I rushed out to get some décor and purchase gifts. I found the cutest 4-foot tree and knew the perfect place to put it in our home, so I decorated the house with all of the items I'd found. You know that everything is picked over the closer you get to the date of Christmas. but I remember Mike sitting back on the sofa and telling me how much he loved the decorations. I laughed.

"No, I'm serious. I really like and appreciate what you've done," said Mike. I thanked him with a smile and gave him a kiss.

We enjoyed Christmas day at home and had some friends come over for dinner. Then on the 28th of

December, my parents, my brother and his family, my adopted mom, and my adopted sister brought Christmas to us. It was awesome! We were all so happy just being together. Mike told me how special it was that they thought enough of us to go out of their way to come and visit. I agreed. We were humbled by it. The following Saturday evening, January 6th, 2019, our son Devin, Walter (a friend of the family), and Mike's mother came for a visit. We enjoyed their company as well.

Unfortunately, Michael's health continued to decline despite what things looked like on the outside. Michael kept his faith in God. It was such a powerful thing to witness in my husband. I could truly see that he had an intimate relationship with God. This is what I had prayed for years ago and it happened in ways I couldn't have even imagined.

During one of our visits to the doctor post-surgery, the doctor delivered news that the tumors were growing. The doctor continued to speak about the unfavorable medical report, but Mike interrupted and said, "I don't mean any harm or disrespect to you doctor, but I'm rebuking everything you're saying to me right now. I choose to trust God." Wow! I was so proud of Mike. He undoubtedly and unflinchingly confessed his belief and trust in God to the doctor. That should be a lesson to all of us. No matter the circumstance, God is in control. God has the final say. We must trust in knowing this.

On February 8th, 2019, Mike and I traveled to the doctor at Duke University Cancer Center for what we thought would be a chance to potentially hear about some other treatment options. When the nurse took Mike's blood pressure, it was around 50 over 80. Like, hold up. Stop the presses. The nurse immediately contacted the doctor and after several attempts at checking his vitals, Mike was rushed to the hospital. Everything began to happen so fast. The doctor told me that Mike was in very critical condition and to contact family to have them come. My heart dropped. I begin to pray and pray and pray. I started making the phone calls to family. With no hesitation, they were on their way from near and far. The news of Mike being in the hospital spread and as the days went on more friends and family came to the hospital to visit. The outpouring of love was amazing. Mike was sooooo incredibly happy to see everyone. Although Mike's vitals had improved some, the doctors informed us that they would not be able to administer any more treatments and had run out of options. Mike was in the ICU for a few days and discharged from the hospital on February 12th. Despite what we saw, we kept praying to God for a miracle. Mike remained positive.

We continued our fight for Michael's survival. We went back to the local oncologist's office where the nurses and the staff were positively wonderful the day after Mike was discharged. I truly knew in my heart that they cared for me and Michael. They hadn't seen Mike since his surgery, so I could tell from their faces that they were all saddened by his current condition. Still, they remained professional and courteous. They gave me and Mike a beacon of light to hold onto.

On February 15th, our Pastor in Virginia hosted a noonday prayer call. On this particular day, he unmuted the call so that people could ask for prayer. This was something that he had not done before. Mike requested prayer for me and the kids. I thought that was odd because I knew he needed prayer. "Aren't you going to ask for prayer?" I said. Mike shook his head no and I was kind of taken aback by that.

When we got off the prayer call Mike said, "I just want you and the kids to be ok."

"Don't start to lose faith" I pleaded. "God's got you."

"I know," Michael replied.

Looking back on that conversation, I think that was one of Mike's subtle ways of preparing me for what was to come. When I think back, I can see clues that while he was hoping for the best, he was also preparing for his transition. He would often tell me how strong I was. He told me he was proud to have me as his wife. He told me that he appreciated me being with him every step of the way. He told me I was doing a great job with the kids. He told me he was so proud of me for being able to take care of him and still do well in my business. We discussed where he wanted to have his funeral, who he wanted to have do the eulogy, the clothes he wanted to be laid to rest in, and where he wanted to be buried. I remember crying when we had that unavoidable conversation. He held my hand and told me I was strong. I didn't feel strong at all. I told him I needed him and the kids needed him too. I encouraged him to keep fighting, and he did for as long as he could.

Dear God, Please help me...

"Blessed are those who mourn, for they will be comforted."
Matthew 5:4

Chapter 4

March 1st, 2019: A Glimpse of Comfort

I sat on the edge of the bed in my old bedroom at my parents' house. I continued to hear the doorbell ringing downstairs. Family and friends were gathering together to go to the church. The funeral home directors would be arriving soon to take us there for Michael's homegoing service.

My stomach was in knots. I had mustered up enough energy to make sure that the kids were straight and to get myself dressed. But barely. I still couldn't believe this was happening. Why were we going through this?

The knock on the bedroom door startled me. "Come in," I said. My mother and brother were at the door.

"They're here. It's time to go," said my mom.

My brother looked at me and reassuringly promised, "It's going to be okay."

"I don't want to go," I said. "I don't want to do this."

"None of us do. But we will get through this togeth-er," my mom said solemnly.

I took a deep breath and walked into the hallway. My father motioned for me to follow him. He went down the stairs first, followed by my mother, my brother, and me. With each step down the stairs, the tears threatened to boil over and I began to cry. The kids were already downstairs waiting with family. Under the direction of the funeral home attendants, they said a prayer and then we were directed to the funeral limos. It felt like I was moving in slow motion. This just seemed like a bad dream that I just couldn't wake up from.

Moments later we arrived at the church. I loved and still love it—and not because of its beautiful outward frame. I love this church because of the people who at-tend. The people, from the senior pastor on down to the congregation, had become a part of our extended fami-ly. This was our home church. When we lived in Virginia before moving to North Carolina we attended, served, and fellowshipped here on a regular basis. Michael had requested to be brought home to Virginia and have our pastor do the eulogy. I was glad we were able to manifest his wishes.

Family and friends lined up to go inside for the fu-neral procession. I felt so weak. I placed my sunglasses over my eyes. I was drowning in tears. I could hear people talking but the voices began to sound groggy like I was swimming under water. The funeral directors began to line the family up two by two, and we were led to the doorways of the church. The pastors and ministers walked down the aisle first. Then, it was time for me to walk down the aisle.

My father walked me down the aisle just like he had done almost 14 years prior on my wedding day. This time, however, family and friends were walking behind us and Mike wasn't standing at the end waiting for me. My husband was laying lifeless in a casket. How could this be? I know our vows said 'til death do we part, but why did death come so soon? It felt like we were just getting started. *This can't be the end? It ends like this?* I thought to myself. Today, the aisle felt extremely long. "Please let me make it Lord," I prayed internally. My legs felt like they were going to give out again just like they did when I first found out about Mike's passing. I arrived at the casket. With the help of the funeral director and my dad, I removed my sunglasses.

Through the warm tears streaming down my face, I stared at the frame of what used to be my husband's body. I just wanted to scream at the top of my lungs. I wanted Mike to wake up. I wanted this to just be a bad joke that Mike was playing on me (we would often play jokes on each other and the kids). I felt like I was going to vomit. I managed to walk away from the casket and sit down. The kids were right behind me. I watched our three kids view their dad's body. Our children loved their dad and he loved them back very much. They were all so sad. I wished there was something I could have done to take away their pain. I felt so helpless. I cried as family and friends continued to walk by and view Michael's remains.

Once the last person viewed the body, my dad and one of the funeral directors escorted me up front to cover up the body so that the morticians could close the casket. "This is it," I said to myself. *This is the last time I will ever see Michael's body. This is the last time I will get to cover him as I often did with a blanket when he would fall asleep on the couch or on the floor* (he loved taking naps on the floor). "God!" I cried out loud with a faint voice. My father began to cry. I moved my father's hand from the casket and watched as the morticians closed it for the very last time. My father and I were escorted back to our seats. It seemed as if my heart stopped beating for a few minutes. I was motionless and I couldn't hear a sound.

During the service I was in a daze, zoning in and zoning out as the ceremony proceeded. I know that I spoke and gave tribute to Mike, but I don't remember much of what I said. I remember staring at the closed casket for moments at a time.

We arrived at the cemetery and I watched our friends and family get out of their cars to walk to the gravesite. I watched the pall bearers carry Mike's remains to place it on the vault that lowers caskets into the ground. The limo door opened for me and the rest of the family to get out of the car. It was raining lightly. We were seated and the closing service began. I was numb, sad, and felt helpless. Way more than anything else I just wanted to take the pain away from my children, the oldest being 25 years old, my daughter at 13 years old, and our youngest son at 9 years old. I just hurt so badly for them. The conclusion of the service at the cemetery was very short. I remember the silent tears streaming down my face as I stared at the casket and heard the words, "...ashes to ashes, dust to dust..." I honestly thought that I was going to throw up. My stomach was so queasy and I felt my mouth watering up. "God, please don't let me vomit...please don't let me vomit," I begged quietly to myself. Then I remember hearing the words, "...this concludes the service for...." There were a lot of family and friends that came over to hug and encourage me and the immediate family members who were sitting down. After a few minutes, I was escorted back to the limo through the crowd of friends and loved ones. As I walked, the warm tears streaming down my cheeks mingled with the cool rain, interconnected as if it were providing a glimpse of comfort from heaven. Somehow, I could sense that Mike was with me right then and there. I can't really put it into words.

"Trust in the Lord with all your heart and lean not unto your own understanding. Acknowledge Him in all your ways and He will direct your path" Proverbs 3:5-6. This was Mike's favorite passage of biblical scripture. He even had it as a wallpaper on his cell phone. God's word says that to be absent from the body is to be present with the Lord. I truly believe that Mike lives on and when God calls me home, I will see him again. I too, am leaning on this passage. I don't understand why all of this had to happen, but I trust that God has a plan.

Throughout this journey, I have found myself reading and reflecting on the book of Ruth in the bible. For those of you who may not be familiar with this passage I will give a quick background description.

The book of Ruth (Ruth 1:1-5 NIV) opens with hardship, suffering, loss, and grief.

"Now it came about in the days when the judges

governed, that there was a famine in the land. And a certain man of Bethlehem in Judah went to sojourn in the land of Moab with his wife and his two sons. And the name of the man was Elimelech, and the name of his wife, Naomi; and the names of his two sons were Mahlon and Chilion, Ephrathites of Bethlehem in Judah. Now they entered the land of Moab and remained there. Then Elimelech, Naomi's husband, died; and she was left with her two sons. And they took for themselves Moabite women as wives; the name of the one was Orpah and the name of the other Ruth. And they lived there about ten years. Then both Mahlon and Chilion also died; and the woman was bereft of her two children and her husband."

What a way to start off a story. In our society today, Naomi would have been considered an older widow whereas Ruth would be considered a young widow. Either way, becoming a widow in biblical times left women isolated and destitute because of the heavy social and cultural reliance on the husband as sole provider. Where would their futures lie? Naomi left her hometown with her husband only for him to pass away. Then ten years later, both of her sons would pass away leaving Naomi with her two daughters-in-law. It is possible that Naomi may have felt some type of security knowing that her two sons could still provide for her. So, to be faced with the death of both sons must have been like tearing open an old wound and allowing the blood to spill out freely. She had to cope with her grief while figuring out how to survive. In those days, pension plans didn't exist and there was no such thing as survivor's benefits. Due to her age, we can also conclude that her parents were no longer living, leaving her with no immediate family with whom she could seek refuge. She was also faced with the prospect of taking care of her two daughters-in-law.

Naomi, although not sure of her plan, decided to return home to Bethlehem. She encouraged Ruth and Orpah to return to their families in Moab. Orpah took Naomi's advice and returned to her family. Ruth however, clung to Naomi and pleaded to stay with her: *"Entreat me not to leave thee, or to return from following after thee: for whither thou goest, I will go; and where thou lodgest, I will lodge: thy people shall be my people, and thy God my God; Where thou diest, will I die, and there will I be buried: the Lord do so to me, and more also, if ought but death part thee and me"* (Ruth I: I6,17 KJV). Ruth's words to Naomi describe the type of bond and enduring love that the two had for each other. It was a love based off of mutual respect and support and was free of toxicity: a true friendship, to say the least. Naomi agreed that Ruth could return to Bethlehem with her. They arrived in Bethlehem as the barley harvest was beginning.

In order to provide for the two of them, Ruth went out into the fields to pick up leftover grain behind the harvesters. As it turned out, she was working in a field that belonged to Boaz, a relative on Naomi's husband's side of the family. Ruth found favor with Boaz and he advised her not to glean—that is, not to collect the leftovers—in anyone else's field. By the end of her first day gleaning she had about 30 pounds of barley to take home to Naomi. Naomi was excited to see how much Ruth had gathered and asked whose field Ruth had gleaned in. Ruth told Naomi that it was Boaz's field, and Naomi informed Ruth that Boaz was their close relative and one of their guardian-redeemers.

Boaz was not next in line to be Ruth's kinsman redeemer. He went to the relative who was next in line and advised him of the situation. The relative did not want to marry Ruth, therefore Boaz and the relative arranged for Boaz to become Ruth's kinsman redeemer. Ruth and Boaz married and they had a son named Obed who would go on to become the grandfather of King David and part of Jesus's lineage. Wow! Powerful!

You see, Ruth didn't come from a wealthy background. She didn't come from a family that had influential positions in the community. In our present-day society, Ruth would likely be considered a regular lower- to middle- class citizen. However, because of her obedience, submissiveness, bravery, and integrity, God used her in ways that she probably never imagined, and her story is still being told today.

Some of the things I take away from this story are:

Aha Moment #1- In some of the most challenging and devasting times in our lives there is still hope. It is absolutely pulverizing to lose a spouse. It is often very difficult to make wise decisions during this time. Ruth left everything that she was familiar with in her hometown to move to a foreign town with her mother-in-law although she knew no one. Ruth chose to submit to Naomi's God and to Naomi. This proved to be a very wise decision. Neither Ruth nor Naomi knew how they would survive, yet they had hope that by moving back to Bethlehem, somehow everything would work out.

When life hits you so hard that it literally knocks the wind out of you, it's definitely hard to find hope for the future. It's easy to feel like you could just lay in the bed with the sheets over your head and quit moving forward. I encourage you to find even the tiniest amount of hope and faith during these times. Hebrews 11:1 (NIV) says, *"Now faith is confidence in what we hope for and assurance about what we do not see."* Having faith and finding hope are the keys to getting through moment to moment. Notice that I did not say day to day. When you're facing these types of difficult challenges, it is easier to take things in smaller pieces like hour by hour or even minute by minute. Allow yourself time as you keep moving forward.

Aha Moment #2 – Having selfless love for others may not be easy but can be immensely rewarding. Ruth's commitment to move with Naomi was a selfless act of love and kindness. It was an amazing example of the love of Christ. Ruth had no idea that due to her selfless act of love and kindness, she would become part of the lineage of Jesus Christ. What an absolutely outstanding reward!

Aha Moment #3 – Be known for your integrity. Having integrity is doing the right thing even when no one is watching. Ruth is a great example of a woman who had great character. Although she was a foreigner in Bethlehem, her positive reputation proceeded her. In Ruth 2:11; 3:10-11 (KJV) Boaz acknowledges Ruth in this regard:

...It hath fully been shewed me, all that thou hast done unto thy mother in law since the death of thine husband: and how thou hast left thy father and thy mother, and the land of thy nativity, and art come unto a people which thou knewest not here-tofore...Blessed be thou of the Lord, my daughter; for thou hast shewed more kindness in the latter end than at the beginning, inasmuch as thou fol-lowedst not young men, whether poor or rich. And now, my daughter, fear not; I will do to thee all that thou requirest: for all the city of my people doth know that thou art a virtuous woman.

Ruth went well above what she could have done and decided to follow and take care of her mother-in-law. Ruth's actions spread across the town and she became known as a virtuous woman. That's something we should all strive for.

Aha Moment #4 – God uses ordinary people for HIS purpose. Ruth, as mentioned before, didn't come from a wealthy background or a hierarchy of leaders. She was considered ordinary by her peers.

Ruth was a childless widow struggling with poverty. In those days, women were considered barren if they could not have children. Think about it—Ruth was married to her husband for ten years and did not conceive. It's possible that she may have even given up on the possibility of having children. Anyone looking on from the outside would never have guessed that God would use her as an instrumental figure in the lineage of Christ. Yet, He did it!

Ruth's story reminds us that no matter our pasts or how difficult our current circumstances, we are still valuable to God. God can take what we think is hopeless and turn it into something miraculous. God is amazing!

The book of Ruth has definitely been a book that I refer back to again and again. Especially during those tough moments. You know, when I was single prior to being married, I read the book of Ruth with my thoughts focused on finding my "Boaz"—meaning that I hoped that God would lead me to my husband. Now, I read the story of Ruth as a reminder that God is my strength and my redeemer. There is healing and hope for my future if I trust in Him and the same holds true for all of you.

Dear God, This is an emergency! I'm a widow and a mom. This is unimaginable.

"Come to me, all you who are weary and burdened, and I will give you rest."

Matthew 11:28 NIV

Chapter 5

March 4th, 2019: The Reality of Being Instantly Single

"Now what…?" I thought to myself. I was very grateful for the outpouring of love from family, friends and community near and far. It was now time for the kids and I to return to North Carolina. There was a lot that needed to be done and a lot of hard decisions that needed to be made.

When a person is grieving, they are generally told to try not to make any concrete decisions. Well, in my situation that wasn't the case. The school year would end in June. Would we stay in North Carolina or move closer to family? Among other things, we needed to move out of the place where we were currently living.

"I've finished packing the car," I told my parents and my kids.

"Are you sure you don't want us to go back with you?" asked dad.

"I'm sure. I don't want you to make that trip and then have to turn around and come back," I said.

"Okay. Well we will be checking on y'all," said dad.

We said our see you laters and the kids and I drove back to North Carolina. Halfway back, I began to think that I should have taken my parents up on their offer. But it was too late now. I had to keep driving towards North Carolina. I was fine until I parked the car at home. I woke up the kids up. We unpacked the car and closed the front door. The kids went upstairs. The house was very quiet. I stood in the room where Mike worked from home and I looked around at the computer and his headset equipment. I started crying, loudly and uncontrollably. The kids came downstairs and we all cried together. We cried for a long time.

Being a widowed single mother is different from being a single mother or a divorced single mother. It's different insofar as widowed single mothers have been married before but no longer have living spouses. A single mom is a mother who has never been married, and their current or ex-partner can very well still play a vital role in raising the children. A single divorced mother is a mom who has been married before, but her ex-husband still lives and still has the potential to help with the kids. Being a widowed single mom HAPPENS IN AN

INSTANT. The status is abrupt. It's a club that no one wants to belong.

Not only are there suddenly new challenges to contend with as a parent, but there are also new challenges with maintaining friendships. You go from being married and getting invited to go out as a couple with your married friends to—intentionally or unintentionally—getting left out and left behind. Sometimes friends are okay with you talking about your deceased spouse, but at others, these awkward moments of silence can arise because people don't know what to say to you or because talking about it would make them uncomfortable. It's easy to find yourself quickly changing the subject to make others feel comfortable while internally slipping into a more isolated place. I didn't realize that I was doing it at first. I attended a grief counseling session and there we discussed how to cope with this type of scenario.

How do we get back to who we were before the death of our spouse?

How do we get back to who we were before the death of our spouse? It takes time. We must, with God's help, go through the pain of finding *us* and taking care of *us*. It's not always cut and dry, either. One minute you think you're fine and the next minute you're crying or angry or very sad. Sometimes you may even feel guilty about small things like not cooking dinner for the kids. Side note: y'all, let me tell you. I probably went for days, maybe even a few months at a time buying fast food or eating cereal for dinner. It just seemed like the thought of me cooking was unbearable. The struggle was real. I struggled with my new status as a widowed mom. I was used to making dinners for the four of us. Mentally and emotionally it was so hard for me to get past this. Each day we purchased fast food for dinner I felt horrible yet relieved that I didn't have to make it. Within the first few weeks after Mike had passed, I remember attempting to purchase items to cook dinner from the grocery store. I went into the store and started walking down the aisles and had an uncontrollable breakdown of silent tears. I just couldn't do it at that moment. I had to leave the store. I was triggered by not needing to buy certain foods specifically for Mike anymore and it left me in tears.

I am so very grateful for God's grace in surrounding me with people who I describe as my angel friends on earth for just showing up with meals or restaurant gift cards. You see, when our family moved to North Carolina, it took a while before we found a church where we as a family could grow and fellowship. But we finally did, and in this moment, their support was invaluable. They prayed for our family during the journey and held a Griefshare ministry that helped tremendously. My friend also invited me to attend a bible class at her church. I grew so much from this bible class that I decided to be a part of another one. During this class, I shared my husband's diagnosis and that despite the circumstances, we were still believing and trusting in God for a miracle. The women in the ministry just showed up for me and the kids. They put a cooler on my front porch and weekly they filled it with meals that I could just put into the oven; or otherwise, they would send cards with gift cards to restaurants inside of them. How amazing! I still praise God for sending these wonderful ladies my way to help me and my kids at a very difficult time.

I had to realize that this is an inescapably emotional journey. If you're reading this and have experienced the loss of your spouse or a loved one, understand and remember that it is an emotional journey. You know what? It's okay. It's okay to simply not be okay as long as you're moving in a direction where you will be one day. We will make it through, one moment at a time. God is close to the brokenhearted, and he wants to rescue us. He sees our hurt and knows our pain. He truly understands when we feel like we are drowning. Allow God to rescue you.

~

Stages of Grief

During the eulogy at Mike's funeral service, our pastor, Reverend Kevin Swann, Dr. Min. reminded us that there are cycles of grief. The emotional cycles of grief include denial, anger, bargaining, depression, and acceptance—often but not always in that order—according to a theory developed by psychiatrist Elisabeth Kubler-Ross. Let's take a look at each stage of her theory.

Denial

Denial can help us to minimize the overwhelming pain of loss. As we process the reality of our loss, we are also trying to survive emotional, mental, and sometimes physical pain. It can be hard to believe that we have truly lost an important person in our lives, especially when we may have just spoken with this person earlier that day, the previous day, or the previous week. During this stage of grief, our realities have shifted completely and we sometimes cannot—or will not—accept it. Adjusting to this new reality takes time for us to process.

Anger

Anger is probably a much more common response than you may realize. Adjusting to the reality that our spouse or loved one is no longer there can be very challenging, and sometimes, people will try to find someone or something else to blame for their loss. It's okay to be angry. However, it's important to recognize that ultimately, God has the final say. He knew when we would be born into this world and he knows when we will leave this world. Anger can be one of the first things we experience with our emotions at the time of loss. We have to be careful not to get stuck in this angry stage because it can lead to isolation, exacerbated by a reputation for being unapproachable. Let's face it—grieving is tough and at one point or another, we could all benefit from connection and comfort from others.

Bargaining

When coping with loss, it is common to feel so desperate that you are willing to do almost anything to alleviate or minimize the pain. Losing a loved one can lead us to consider any way that we might avoid the current pain or the pain anticipated from the loss. There are many ways we may try to bargain.

Bargaining usually comes in the form of promises,

such as:
- "I promise to be better if you will let _____ live."
- "God, if you can heal _____, I will turn my life around."
- "I'll never get angry again if you can stop _____ from dying."

The feeling of helplessness that comes with loss can lead us to react in protest by bargaining, which gives us a perceived sense of control over something that feels so out of control. During the bargaining stage of grief, regretful thinking may begin to enter our minds. Please don't get stuck on these thoughts. You will have to learn how to release these thoughts when they come over you, and to make internal peace with the things that were or were not said or done with your loved one.

Depression

According to Britannica, depression, in psychology, "is a mood or emotional state that is marked by feelings of low self-worth or guilt and a reduced ability to enjoy life." During the process of grief, there comes a time when our imaginations calm down and we slowly start to look at the reality of our present situations. The loss feels more present. In those moments, we tend to turn inward as the sadness grows. We might find ourselves retreating, being less sociable, and less frequently reaching out to others about what we are going through. Although this is a very natural stage of grief, dealing with depression after the loss of a loved one can be extremely isolating. It may even be very difficult to communicate what you are experiencing to others. Attending individual counseling sessions with a grief counselor or small group grief counseling sessions may be helpful for you.

Acceptance

During the acceptance stage of grief, we finally come to terms with the reality of our loss. This doesn't mean that we no longer experience the pain that comes with grief; it simply means that we are no longer living in the stagnation of disbelief that our love one has transitioned.

According to an article by Jodi Clarke in Verywell Mind,

> As we consider the five stages of grief, it is important to note that people grieve differently and you may or may not go through each of these stages, or experience each of them in order. The lines of these stages are often blurred—we may move from one stage to the other and possibly back again before fully moving into a new stage.

In addition, there is no specific time period suggested for any of these stages. Someone may experience the stages fairly quickly, such as in a matter of weeks, where another person may take months or even years to move through to a place of acceptance. Whatever time it takes for you to move through these stages is perfectly normal.

Your pain is unique to you, your relationship to the person you lost is unique, and the emotional processing can feel different to each person. It is acceptable for you to take the time you need and remove any expectation of how you should be performing as you process your grief."

I honestly don't know how anyone makes it living this life without God. I mean, He is the one that created us and knows what He has in store for us. It just makes sense to have a relationship with him. Through this experience, however, I also understand what it's like to be angry with God. I can relate to Naomi in the story of Ruth when she told the woman in her hometown, *"Don't call me Naomi... call me Mara, because the Almighty has made my life very bitter. I went away full, but the Lord has brought me back empty. Why call me Naomi? The Lord has afflicted me; the Almighty has brought misfortune upon me."* Ruth 1:20-21 (NIV).

I had the hard conversations with God. I told God that I was angry with Him. I told Him that I was mad because he took the kids' father away from them. I was mad because he took my husband away. We were finally in a good place. I was angry because we didn't get a chance to live out our hopes and dreams. I was angry because Mike prayed for others, especially the lady with lung cancer throughout her body, and God healed her but didn't do the same for Mike. I was angry that God answered my prayers for marriage only to take my husband away. I was angry, angry, Angry!

Accordingly, I have to be transparent with you and I hope you won't judge me, because I'm not proud of this. After his death, I went through a period when I didn't like hearing about other people's testimonies because God didn't heal Mike. I remember feeling jealous when God healed others—specifically of cancer. I know it wasn't right. From the bottom of my heart, I knew I was wrong. I just had to be real with God. I believe that God wanted me to be this way. Not angry. Just real. That's the only way we can authentically have a relationship with God.

God is our Father. When you think about it, when we were children, we would sometimes get mad at our parents if they didn't do something we wanted them to do. I don't know if your parents were like mine, but our parents couldn't have cared less if my brother and I were angry with them. Their eternal refrain to us was, "You'll be alright." It's funny because now I tell my kids the same thing. Eventually, we got over being angry with our parents and moved forward. Just like our parents, God can handle our anger. He just doesn't want us to get stuck in it.

One day when I was having an internal anger session, I felt like I was reprimanded or hit upside my head by God. Not physically. However, I was *shook*. I sensed God saying to me, "Monica, this is not about you! Stop doubting my faithfulness just because I don't come at your beck and call! I'm not your bell boy or a genie. I AM GOD! I don't move according to your time. I move according to MY plan. I am in control. This is about MY GLORY! Your focus should be on trusting and worshipping me." Whew! I was chastised that moment. I truly had to humble myself. The nerve of me! How dare I place myself higher than I ought to?

Along this journey of widowhood, I have found myself entering into a deeper relationship with God. I know in my heart that God has my best interests and the kids' best interests at heart. Romans 8:28 (NIV) states,

"And we know that in all things God works for the good of those who love him, who have been called according to his purpose." While at the current moment, I do not see why things happened in the way that they did, I do trust that God has a greater purpose. I believe God has a bigger plan. I asked God for forgiveness. I had to humble myself and remember that He has all power and authority over my life. I'm grateful that He's a forgiving God. Through this grief, I find myself talking and praying to Him frequently. That's exactly where He wants all of us to be. Looking to and finding strength in His guidance and His will. He continues to open doors for the kids and me in countless ways. I am in awe of Him!

Taking on the responsibility of both parents

"Mommy, I'm going to be late for school!" "Mommy don't be mad, I forgot I have a project that's due and I need to get the materials. The project is due tomorrow." "Mommy, can I hang out with my friends this weekend?" "Mommy, can I have a play date?" "Mommy, what's for dinner?" "Mommy…" "Mommy…" "Mommy!!"

The role of being both parents in an instant can be stressful all by itself. For the most part, my kids are good kids. I love them wholeheartedly! I don't always get it right. Sometimes I feel like I'm re-enacting one of the scenes from the movie "Bad Moms" *cringes*. For example, I can't stand when I'm late for an appointment or for an event or anything that the kids and I are supposed to be doing. The last stretch of the school year and my time management were not in sync. I admit that I truly just wanted to just lay in bed with the covers over my head and pretend that school did not exist. It seemed like most mornings I was getting out of the house late and speeding to get my son to school (my daughter went to school later so when I took her, she was on time). Some mornings I would get him there before the bell rang, however, a lot more of those mornings, he arrived after the bell rang. Ugh! Thank goodness for understanding teachers and school staff who were aware of our situation. They were a BIG help!

Mike and I worked together with the kids and we had a routine of who would do what with them. After he had taken ill his role lessened significantly, but we were both praying and hoping for the best. We believed that he would be healed and get back to working and doing for the kids like before. Not having him around makes it very challenging to take a break from the day-to-day responsibilities of taking care of the kids and running errands. It's important to surround yourself with a village of people that can serve as a support system for you and your children. This is one of the reasons why I decided to move closer to family. It has proven to be very beneficial.

Broken sleep

Another thing I had to come to terms with was the suddenness of being the only adult in my home. It was a struggle and at times can still be a struggle. Yes, Mike sometimes traveled for his job and he occasionally went on weekend trips with friends, but I knew that he would be returning. Things are different now. I went through a very long period of broken sleep and still do at times. Sometimes I would only sleep about 40 minutes to an hour at a time. Broken sleep is no joke. This was a challenge. I found that I could sleep better if the kids and I stayed with my parents or my brother and sister. Of course, this was only a temporary fix. I had to pray about it, exercise, read books, drink herbal tea, and listen to sermons and soft music to help me sleep. The broken sleep added to the high level of stress I was already enduring. I had to make self-care my priority.

The Importance of Self-care

According to Oxford, self-care is defined as the following:

noun

1. the practice of taking action to preserve or improve one's own health.

    "autonomy in self-care and insulin administration"

o   the practice of taking an active role in protecting one's own well-being and happiness, in particular during periods of stress.

"expressing oneself is an essential form of self-care"

Becoming a widow—or losing a loved one in general—can really take a negative toll on your physical body. Not to mention the struggle if you were a caregiver prior to your loved one's passing. Your body will feel the stress. According to WebMD, some of the physical symptoms of grief include headaches, stomach pain, fatigue, dry mouth, nausea, loss of appetite, and even chest pain. These symptoms shouldn't be taken lightly.

What causes these physical symptoms? According to WebMD,

> ...research reveals the powerful effects grief can have on the body. Grief increases inflammation, which can worsen health problems you already have and cause new ones. It batters the immune system, leaving you depleted and vulnerable to infection. The heartbreak of grief can increase blood pressure and the risk of blood clots. Intense grief can alter

the heart muscle so much that it causes broken heart syndrome—a form of heart disease with the same symptoms as a heart attack.

Stress links the emotional and physical aspects of grief. The systems in the body that process physical and emotional stress overlap, and emotional stress can activate the nervous system as easily as physical threats can. When stress becomes chronic, increased adrenaline and blood pressure can contribute to chronic medical conditions.

Research shows that emotional pain activates the same regions of the brain as physical pain. This may be why painkilling drugs ranging from Tylenol to opioids have been shown to ease emotional pain.

Implementing self-care should become a priority. It's perfectly fine to take care of yourself. I have to do it intentionally. It is definitely an ongoing process but is truly necessary for your health. It's time to love on yourselves! I'm so serious right now. Especially if you're the only parent present in your children's lives. They may not realize fully how much they need you, but they do. It's important that we do everything that we can on our end to take care of them. In order to do that, we have to make taking care of ourselves a top priority!

Here are 10 things that I have put in place to jump-start my personal self-care. This is not a prescription for you. Rather, I am sharing these suggestions with you because they have helped me. See which ones, if any, resonate with you and give them chance to see how it works!

1 - Read and Meditate on God's Word

I make time in the morning to read a devotional or a passage of scripture from the bible. It helps me to start my day off with a clear and positive perspective. Meditating on God's word throughout the day is a reminder to me that I'm not doing life by myself. It helps me to fight off those negative thoughts that creep into my mind at times, trying to discourage me.

#2 – Sing and Dance

I love to sing and dance! Always have. One of my goals for the year is to just simply remember to sing and dance each day. Yes, I love the Lord. Yes, I love to sing songs of praise and worship. I also like to mix it up. I like to throw in R&B, Hip Hop, and Classics from the 60s, 70s, 80s, and 90s. Have fun!!

#3 – Write in A Journal

Writing in a journal is therapeutic. It's a way to communicate with God or perhaps even with your loved one who has graduated to Heaven. Journaling is also a good way to communicate with your kids. For example, you could use a journal for each child. Write something in the journal to your child and slip it under their pillow at night. Have your child write back to you and put it under your pillow the next day. It's important for your children to have different ways to communicate positively with you.

#4 – Breathing Exercises

I have implemented breathing exercises when I start getting frustrated or overwhelmed. Breathing exercises can be done in various ways. I like to take a deep breath in and slowly exhale for about eight seconds. I repeat this about three to five times in a row. These breathing exercises help me to relax and gain focus.

#5 – Drink Plenty of Water

When going through grief and experiencing some of the stages of grief we discussed earlier, you may not realize how much or how little water you're in-putting into your body. Our bodies need plenty of water to begin with, but when you add tears to the mix it becomes even more important to drink water. Since Mike has passed away, I have moments where I cry a lot. Research shows that excessive amounts of the stress hormone and cortisol are produced in grief and crying. This makes it difficult to sleep and concentrate. Drinking more water can help flush away the toxins and replenish us when we feel like we're in a fog.

#6 – Treat Yourself

Do something for you that you love! Perhaps it's taking a walk, going to a movie, getting a massage, shopping, going to a festival, going to your favorite restaurant, painting, getting a manicure and pedi-cure, getting a facial, going to a vineyard, or going to a concert. Think about those things that you know you like to do or things you have been wanting to check out. Then DO THEM!! You deserve to enjoy your life!!

#7 – Exercise

Now, I have a confession to make. I have a love/

hate relationship with exercise. You see, I feel really accomplished after a workout, yet getting to the gym and actually working out is my downfall a lot of times. Ugh. I have joined a gym and I don't like wasting money, so I am working on different ways to win this battle. Exercise benefits the brain by increasing blood flow and focus. Research says that regular exercise can help relieve many of the physical symptoms of grief we discussed. You might consider joining a gym or a running group or a local yoga studio to make exercise part of your self-care rhythm.

#8 – Schedule Time with Friends and Family

Since Mike's passing, it has been so easy to find myself not wanting to be with other people. Not because I don't like people. I love people. I find myself not wanting to be around others because I don't want to be the one to bring the mood down. I enjoy being around people who exude a positive and upbeat energy. I know we all have our moments where we may be going through some challenging times and need a friend to talk to. When it comes to me—and I know that I'm not alone in what I'm about to say—I just don't want to be the one talk about the true depth of my ongoing sadness. I know that is not healthy. I am grateful for the friends and family that reach out to check on me. Now, I purposely schedule time to either call or go out with my friends and family. This is so important when it comes to self-care. God did not create and design us to do life by ourselves here on earth. We need that balance.

#9 – Make an Appointment to See Your Doctor

The impact of grief and stress can cause health issues. Grief is a natural reaction to loss, and is not an illness itself, however, it would be a good time just to get checked out by your doctor. This check-up will give you the opportunity to attend to any pre-existing health conditions that the stress of grief could negatively impact.

#10 – Give Yourself Some Grace

Grief is painful. There is no sugar coating it. It's tough. Treat yourself as you would treat a friend or loved one in words, thoughts, and deeds. Give yourself space to feel the pain of grief, and also give yourself permission to take a break when you need it. Take advantage of taking naps when you can. Also, take a mental health day. Take time out for you.

My list could go on and on. One last thing that I would like to emphasize is how important it is to distance yourself from negativity; that includes negative self-talk and people who are toxic. Negative thoughts about ourselves and/or our circumstances are self-sabotaging. We are God's masterpieces! We are the apples of His eye and are to be treated with dignity and respect from ourselves and others. Always remember that. In Proverbs 4:23 NIV it says, "Above all else, guard your heart, for everything you do flows from it."

What's Next?

I'm a widowed single mom. This status happened in an INSTANT. This was not my dream. This was not my husband's dream. But although things didn't work out as we desired, I do believe that good will come from this pain. On February 23rd, God gave Michael the ultimate healing. Mike graduated into the eternal presence of God. No more sickness, no more stomach aches, no more nausea and vomiting, no more draining fluid from the abdomen, no more excessive weight loss, no more weakness, no more tears. Those of us who believe know that *"To be absent from the body is to be present with the Lord*" (2 Corinthians 5:8 NKJV). I know that Michael is living in God's presence and that he's more than fine.

I believe that God is working behind the scenes on my behalf. What I'm facing right now is going to be used for God's glory. I sincerely believe that I'm going through this trial right now so that I can see more about who God is.

In previous chapters, I've said that this was not the dream. As I move forward in my walk with God, I am beginning to see things differently. I look back at how sickness caused Mike's relationship with God to grow deeper. I see how the trial of sickness caused my marriage to Mike to grow stronger and more intimate. I see how God allowing this sickness to occur brought our family and extended family closer together. I see how this storm of sickness strengthened existing friendships and created new ones. I see how this trial brought a community of family, friends, and strangers together through prayer and acts of service. We pooled our resources together and were of one accord. MAYBE THIS *WAS* THE DREAM. Maybe this was the plan that GOD had for Mike's life. I saw firsthand what God did in Mike's life. Other people, including our kids, were able to see God's movement in Michael's life as well. Glory to God!!! Our afflictions on earth last for a moment. God's glory is eternal.

Each day that I wake up it reminds me that God still has purpose for my life and for His Kingdom. I am not sure where all the pieces will fall. I am just a willing vessel. It's a faith walk. One moment at a time.

Endnotes

1   The names of the nurses have been changed for privacy*

2   Mayo Clinic - Cholangiocarcinoma is a form of cancer that starts in the slender tubes (bile ducts) that carry the digestive fluid bile. Bile ducts connect your liver to your gallbladder and your small intestine. Some people also refer to this as bile duct cancer. Research shows that this type of cancer is uncommon and typically occurs in people aged 50 and older.

3   Memorial Sloan Kettering Cancer Center - states that bile duct cancer is usually asymptomatic until it reaches an advanced stage and has spread to other organs and tissues.

4   Britannica.com - states that bile duct cancer is usually asymptomatic until it reaches an advanced stage and has spread to other organs and tissues.

5   Oxford Dictionary - self-care is defined as the following:
    noun
    1. the practice of taking action to preserve or improve one's own health.

        "autonomy in self-care and insulin administration"
        o   the practice of taking an active role in protecting one's own well-being and happiness, in particular during periods of stress.

        "expressing oneself is an essential form of self-care"

6   Webmd.com – "How Grief Shows Up In Your Body" by Stephanie Hairston

References

Britannica
Dictionary.com
New King James Bible (NKJV)
New International Version (NIV)
Oxford Dictionary
Verywell Mind
WebMD

Author's Note

I pray that this book has encouraged you. This book is part of my testimony. I honestly don't know what I would do if I didn't have God leading and guiding me. I invite you to surrender your life to Him. He'll be there to walk with, talk with, and comfort you. You mean a lot to Him. Now, God doesn't promise that we'll only have good days, however, what He does promise is that He will be with us every step of the way. If you would like to enter into a relationship with God, I invite you to pray this prayer:

Father God, I come to you right now with an open heart and open mind. Please forgive me for my sins. I believe that you sent your only begotten son Jesus to die on the cross for my sins. I believe he rose again on the third day and ask that your holy spirit will abide in me. Thank you, God, for saving me. In Jesus Christ's name I pray. Amen.

If you just prayed this prayer, please let me know so that I may celebrate with you!

About the Author

Monica P. Quinones is an author, speaker, transformation consultant, and coach. She is devoted to helping women entrepreneurs and leaders thrive in living authentically in mind, body, and soul. Monica is determined to slay the negative mindsets that keep women bound in low self-esteem, insecurity, fear, unforgiveness, depression, shame, guilt, and anything else holding them back from living their abundant lives! Monica has a passion for empowering others to succeed through her direct, assertive, and empathetic approach.

Monica is a 2018 Gospel Image Award Nominee in the category of Inspirational Author for her book, *A Cup of Encouragement: 31 Essentials for Uplifting Your Soul.* In this book, she shares powerful insights that will give you the boost you need for starting your day.

For additional resources from Monica, including information for speaking engagements, visit:

www.PoisedSuccess.com

Instagram.com/poised_success

CPSIA information can be obtained
at www.ICGtesting.com
Printed in the USA
LVHW032147081120
671116LV00016B/1351